Georgie Jones writes poems. It is her favourite thing to do. Although she'd like it to be known that a packet[1] of Frazzles and an episode[2] of *Below Deck: Mediterranean* comes an incredibly close second.

A performer by nature and a poet by trade, Georgie is known for her humour and heart. She was a Roundhouse Poetry Slam finalist before joining the Roundhouse Poetry Collective, and subsequently spent a year as Roundhouse Resident Artist. (It's all a bit Roundhouse-centric, this, isn't it? But wait, there's more!)

Her debut spoken-word show *Ish* was commissioned by a consortium of Midlands-based venues and generously supported by the Arts Council. It sold out its preview tour, garnering four- and five-star reviews, and was set to sell equally well during a full UK tour in 2020, until, y'know *(gestures at everything)*.

Undeterred, Georgie took her poetry to social media, where she has built an unexpectedly large and loyal following. An antidote to the algorithm, Georgie's poems struck a chord with audiences across the globe. Her work is widely shared, often quoted and repeatedly returned to.

1 Ten packets. They're only small.
2 Three episodes.

GEORGIE JONES

AND THE WORLD SPINS ANYWAY

Burning Eye

BurningEyeBooks
Never Knowingly
Mainstream

This edition published by Burning Eye Books 2025

www.burningeye.co.uk

@burningeyebooks

Burning Eye Books
15 West Hill, Portishead, BS20 6LG

ISBN 978-1-913958-51-0
Cover photograph by Jack Keyon
Fairground illustrations by LadadikArt licenced via Creative Market

For Smavvy, Mooms and the Farter Starter,
because I'd get in trouble if I didn't.

No, only (half) joking.

Contents

Does Anyone Know What We're Meant to Be Doing?

I have not yet lived enough lifetimes
to know what I am supposed to be doing in this one.

Some days, I wake up
and make myself a lemon water.
Some days, I wake up
and eat a Cornetto
and half a packet of spicy peanuts,
because I'm a grown-up and I can do what I want.

Some days, I am a productivity machine,
a capitalist's wet dream;
I schedule things into Google calendars,
use phrases like *circling back* and *end of play*.
Some days, I lie on the floor
and whisper *oh my god* into the rug for forty-five minutes.
I think this is what they mean when
they talk about balance.

More often than not, I feel directionless,
a compass needle in search of true north,
in need of remagnetisation.
I don't know who decided
adults weren't allowed the bumpers up,
but I would love a little nudge in the right direction.
My body is tired from all the treading water,
my voice is hoarse from all the
    Is this right?
    Is this right?
    Is this right?
I'm asking for validation
with the frequency and persistence
of a Norton AntiVirus alert.

There never comes a reply,
which means I don't know how to tell
if we're doing it right,
but I do know that sometimes
I rollerskate for three minutes without falling over,
and it is wonderful.
I reread 'The Orange' by Wendy Cope
and it is wonderful.
I feed a goat a handful of Jacob's crackers
and, granted, that one's quite specific,
but, you guessed it, it is wonderful.

At half past one, on a school night,
we find ourselves on stage at the Two Brewers
and it is wonderful.
I kiss my friends on the forehead
and it is wonderful.
I wait for the kettle to boil and decide
not to check my phone
and it is wonderful.
We wake up in the wilderness
with cold noses and fresh coffee
and it is wonderful.
The sun sets and my hair smells like saltwater and
say it with me now
it is wonderful.

And it is, isn't it? But, more than that,
it feels like something close
to confirmation.

There are a hundred ways to live a life;
more, probably.
So, as long as you're living,
I figure
you're doing it right.

Right?

When I first started doing poetry (and admitting it out loud), I adopted an intonation you might reserve for confessing you have a rash: sheepish, apologetic, followed by caveats. *Yeah, I do poetry, but not in a wanky way*. By which I suppose I meant 'without tweed elbow patches or excessive use of pathetic fallacy'.

Poetry has a PR problem. Let's just call a spade a spade. It's like cottage cheese or musical improv, in that most people have already decided how they feel about it and, regrettably, it's not looking amazing.

I know, historically, I haven't helped the cause, what with my tendency to side-eye the ancestors. But even when it's going great, even when you've had a video go mildly viral or packed out a venue to its dusty little rafters, people will still tell you they *don't really like poetry.* More often than not, they will later slide into your DMs to confess they *actually didn't mind this one*. I'm like, babes, y'love it! You're a heartbreak and a Moleskine notebook away from writing your own.

If you already write your own, you've likely been told poetry is a hard sell. I've been told this by agents, well-meaning distant relatives and a man I once dated (who, by the way, dived for golf balls as a profession and still considered me the one with frivolous career goals).

But here we are. Persisting. Finding something worth scribbling about in the banal and the beautiful, the ordinary and the overlooked.

I have found poems in parking tickets and badly microwaved meals and the strange, beautiful ache of remembering someone's laugh.

I think poetry is magic (a shocking revelation from the poet, there). It's a kind of magic I genuinely believe in. Not just as an art form, but as a way of looking at the world.

If you're holding this book, maybe we're related and you felt obliged. Maybe you like poetry. Maybe you're trying to sleep with someone who likes poetry.

Whatever the reason, I'm glad you're here. And, who knows, we might make a poetry fan of you yet.

Everything Is Poetry If You're in the Mood for It

I'm on a second date with this guy;
we'd been on a first date and had quite a nice time,
so we organised a second date
(you know how dating works).
Anyway,
this guy is going to *town*
on a little ramekin of aioli.
It's a communal ramekin, by the way.
I just want you to bear that in mind
while you imagine him
scraping the sides with his index finger,
almost knuckle-deep,
twisting it round and then just
(for want of a better word)
rawdogging aioli
into his mouth.
He looks at me and says,
through mouthfuls of garlicky mayonnaise,
Y'know,
not everything is poetry,
and I'm like, uh
(clutching my pearls),
I don't know how to tell you this…

Y'see that moth,
frenzied and full of longing,
the one that's been throwing its little moth body
at the street lamp for the past ten minutes
because it literally can't imagine a world without brightness?
Poetry.

Or d'you remember when the waitress said *ice cold*,
dropped casual similes into conversation

through loose fingers
like dice across a Monopoly board?
Poetry.

The way neither of us have eaten The Last Chip,
but we both keep eyeing it,
watching it get slowly colder,
and doesn't love sometimes exist like that,
occupying the space between what we really want
and what we're willing to take?
That's poetry.

And then he pulls a face
and I'm like oh, calm down,
I'm not saying I'm in love with you,
it's literally a second date,
God forbid a woman talk about metaphor.
Okay, moving swiftly on.

What about the way
people profess they are nursing a tea,
like Earl Grey might need winding or burping
or, at the very least, to be cradled
between compassionate palms?
I mean, that's basically Shakespearean.

What about the way
beetroot stains your fingertips pink,
or almond milk curdles in coffee,
or the sound of floorboards creaking
when nobody's even walking on them,
as if the house just needs to clear its throat?
What about the bus stop
with its wet, warped bench, damp graffiti,
someone's blunt-carved declaration,
I woz ere,
as if being was ever something we had to prove?

And you,
with your aioli devotion,
elbow on the table like you've had a long week,
but there is life in you yet.
It's almost reverent,
how you push, then scrape
and swirl from the curve of the ramekin.
I mean, it's one of the worst things
I've ever sat opposite,
but if I was in the mood,
you might just be poetry too.

As for the rest of it,
the reflection of the moon on the water,
the knowledge that in Sweden they have a specific word for it
and the word is *mångata*
which literally translates to mean *moon street*.
I mean, come on!
The way the fridge knocks its little light on
every time you open the door,
or the half-second before a kiss,
or IKEA's Billy bookcase assembly instructions,
which might as well exist
as hieroglyphics for perseverance.
The voice notes you listen to on repeat
or the photos you don't look at
but can't bring yourself to delete
or the way this warm light
is falling on your face
or the fact that light is even something
that can fall, and
the sun is something we can catch,
what is that
if not poetry?

He looks at me. For a long while. Pondering.

Then he goes,
Fair.
Like, sorry, that's his entire response to everything I've just said.
And then,
D'you wanna go somewhere else for one more round?
I know a great wine bar by the Underground.

Wait a minute…

And, reader, I married that man.
Nah, just kidding, literally never saw him again.

A Watched Phone Never Vibrates

I am a calm, evolved person.
I meditate (-ed, once, in June 2020,
but halfway through I got distracted
and started Googling is *Timothée Chalamet short?*).
I am a capable woman,
a sophisticated woman.
I drink cocktails with literal vegetables in them[3].
I own a garlic press.

Having said that,
I must confess, I do also look
at WhatsApp's *last online* feature
like a heartsick Victorian wife,
standing at the cliff edge, unblinking,
awaiting her husband's return.
The only slight difference being
this man is not my husband,
nor is he even on a boat;
he's just in Peckham, not texting me back.

The green dot is a beacon of hope,
the *last seen at 14.32* is a knife to the gut.
He has seen my meme
and not replied, which is fine.
People get busy.
I'm busy.
I need to check on my sourdough starter.
I need to swallow the pain
of knowing that at some point in recent history
we existed in the same digital space,
breathed the same 4G, or whatever,
and he chose ~~violence~~ silence.

3 If olives are a vegetable; otherwise untrue.

I open WhatsApp, have a little check.
Quite quickly close it again.
Open it.
Close it. There are a million explanations, okay.

Reasonable ones.
He's at work.
He's asleep.
He's been kidnapped.
He's being held hostage by a group of men who look identical to him, and it is incredibly confusing for the police.
He didn't find the meme funny.
No, that can't be it.
He's died.
He's fallen in love with someone else.
He's just not that into me.

I open WhatsApp, have a little check.
Quite quickly close it again.
Open it.
Close it.
Open it,
scream into a cushion,
close it. Google
what does it mean when someone is online
but not texting you?

A watched phone never vibrates.
Until… it vibrates.
I leap across the room.
Deliveroo can offer £7 off nachos. Google
best songs to cry to 2025.

I open WhatsApp, have a little check,
quite quickly close it again.
I decide I don't care.

But, no, like, I actually don't this time.
Throw my phone across the room,
to prove it.
It lands on my pillow like a baby bird,
like a tiny sleeping fawn.

I miss it.
I crawl to it.
Open it. Have a little check.
Close it again.
This is incessant. I've become obsessive.
Deep breath. I light a candle.
Decide to become a woman who is above this.
Just quickly, open it, have a little check,
close it again.
Yes. Good. Decide to become a woman who is above this.
I delete WhatsApp.

I wonder if he's aware of how online I've been,
how magnetic I am, with all that glimmering green.
I've just got so many people to message
if you disregard the seventeen unanswered texts,
friends long left on read,
left hanging like party balloons
the morning after,
ignoring people I love
in favour of obsessing
over one who is, at best, indifferent.

I reinstall WhatsApp.
Have a little check.
Last online 14.47.
Are. You. Kidding. Me?

So now I'm eating nachos in bed,
because what else would I do with

a Thursday night and a quiet phone but
drip molten cheese on my pillowcases
as a substitute for closure?
Lick guacamole from my fingertips,
not even wondering
if he's doing the same with somebody else,
slurping pico de gallo from her belly button,
their bodies finding each other
like two hard shell tacos in the packet,
like they invented intimacy.

Open WhatsApp, have a little check.
Quite quickly close it again.

He probably eats his nachos
with a knife and fork, anyway.
Bellend.

Single and Entirely Unbothered About Mingling

Listen, my mother did not break her body open,
did not bleed beneath the cold, white lights,
did not push me into this life,
purple-faced and screaming,
just for me to think
none of it matters unless I am with someone.

She did not carry me through nine months of swollen feet
and petrol station pickle cravings
just so I could sit here at 3am
staring at my phone, like
is Jason from Hinge ever gonna text me back, or… –
just so I could spiral about not being engaged to a man
with nice forearms and a golden retriever,
d'you know what I mean?

Have you ever stood in the middle of your kitchen,
eaten mango straight from the knife
and called it a love story?
Have you ever slept starfish in a bed built for two?
Have you ever walked into a bar alone, ordered a drink,
and let whatever song is playing
wrap its arms around you like a slow dance?
Have you ever held your own shoulders in the shower,
given them a little kiss,
heard your own laugh bounce off the walls of an empty room
and still sound full?

Have you ever felt holy peeling an orange at sunrise,
danced in a dirty T-shirt
for no one but the kitchen tiles?
Have you ever laid in the grass, arms wide,
and let the sun touch its mouth to your cheek?

Have you ever pressed your palm
against a train window,
felt the warmth of your own skin and remembered
you belong to yourself first?
Have you ever sat on the floor,
hands wrapped around a chipped mug,
and forgiven yourself
for all the ways you are still learning?
Counted your own pulse,
just to remind yourself you are still here?
Packed a suitcase
just to prove you could leave at any time?

Maybe I'll fall in love again.
Maybe I won't.
Either way, I will still wake up,
stretch into the morning,
flick the kettle on,
throw open the window,
let the air move through me,
and know I belong.

Okay, so I know what I said. I know I went full *Eat Pray Love* about how singledom is delicious and fulfilling and we should cling to it the way my dad clings to out-of-date yogurt, or the way people in airports cling to neck pillows, despite the obvious social cost.

But something, for me, has shifted since that last page and I must confess that I am, in fact, in love.

Sorry.

I don't know what to tell ya! One minute I was happily queueing up some Olivia Dean to get me through tidying my week-long accumulated floordrobe, and the next, there he was, in a tailored suit and mirrored aviators, stopping me in my tracks.

The heart wants what it wants, and what my heart wants is to profess my undying (and unrequited)[4] love for Pitbull.

4 As far as I know.

Mrs Worldwide

Excuse me,
I might drink a little more than I should tonight,
but it's the only way I might muster
something like courage,
so douse me in Dutch,
make me brave enough to say everything
I could barely catch my breath for sober.

Consider this me living in the moment,
because, for all we know,
we might not get tomorrow.
So tonight, I'd like to write you into endless poems,
devote a hundred lines each to
your smile,
your machismo,
your eyes,
then a hundred lines more
once you pop your little shades off
and I can see what they actually look like.
Take me stateside;
we can stand in the centre of Times Square
tipsy with giddiness,
turn ourselves pink and green and orange
as we drink in the lights, and, like everything else I love,
I can take a picture of you,
with a Kodak, if that would make you happy.

If what you say is true, that
I know you want me
just as much as you know I want you
(wantcha)
then let's just sack the rest of it off.
We can rename our hearts *compass*
and we will never get lost.

We can retrace the footsteps you've left
all over the world,
give them some company.
We could tie a bouquet under their arch,
make me Mrs Worldwide,
Mrs 305,
and I will vow, from here on out,
to always yell *timber* when you go down.[5]

When we grow weary,
when I am grey and your head is as shiny as ever,
when we are ready to lower languor into crumpled sheets,
it won't matter whether we're in a
hotel,
motel
or Holiday Inn;
as long as we're together,
we'll enjoy life.
Dale.

5 Sorry.

I have to tell you something.

I performed 'Mrs Worldwide' at a poetry night, then, in a rare and baffling but completely sublime turn of events, a video of the performance gained a fair bit of traction online. The internet, in all its unpredictable glory, passed it around the circle until the music stopped and the video was in the hands of Pitbull himself.

Can you believe it?!

Bald, beautiful, bilingual Mr Worldwide
saw it (!), shared it (!!), captioned it (!!!):

> *When I was a kid, my father would take me out to recite poems to Cubans who arrived in Miami. It's great to see someone taking my words and turning them into poetry.*
>
> *Thank you, Georgie Jones, and I appreciate you more than you know. Daleeeee!*

Dale indeed. Then, he invited me to his show at the O2(!!!!).

Now, I don't know whether he watched the whole thing. If he did, I'm grateful not to know his thoughts on the 'timber' line. As I write this, the invitation to his show has been extended but tickets have not yet arrived. By the time this book comes out, there may be a part two to this story. Or possibly a cease and desist letter. Either way, it's surely worth coming to a live show (mine, not his) just to find out.

So, look, I'm documenting this here because:
a) what on actual Earth,
b) posterity,
and c) it's not completely impossible that I might actually become Mrs Worldwide, move to Miami and lose my entire personality to fame and/or Pitbull-induced serotonin, in which case this will exist as a little breadcrumb trail back to myself.

Anyway, in the interest of balance, here's another love poem. Less riot, more requited.[6] A lovely slow burn after all that sparkle.

6 As far as I know.

Worst-Case Scenario

I read a book, in which Achilles said to Patroclus,
I would recognise you in total darkness,
were you mute and I deaf.
I would recognise you in another lifetime entirely,
in different bodies, different times.
And I would love you in all of this,
until the very last star in the sky
burnt out into oblivion.

That's nice, isn't it?

But to be honest,
I'd settle for doing laundry with you.
We could take it in turns to be bamboozled
by a fitted sheet,
swear as the elasticated corners
spring free for the fourteenth time.

I wouldn't mind
sitting with you in January's grey,
promising not to leave taxes
until the last minute next year,
knowing full well we are creatures of habit,
of eleventh-hour panic,
so that likely won't change.

I'd like there to be plenty of days
where you settle your scaffolding shoulders
behind my tired sighs.
I'd like to memorise the way you linger
at the window
when the sky is wide and quiet.

And in the mornings,
when our hands are busy with small rituals,

yours in the sink,
washing up last night's couldn't-quite-be-bothereds,
and mine glueing breakfast together,
even in the silence of routine,
we'll build something extraordinary.

So, while I am certain we are destined
for greater adventure than this,
if our worst-case scenario culminates in
coffee always brewing
and music always on,
well, I think that sounds quite nice, actually.

A Haiku About Kissing

Leaned in too quickly,
missed your mouth, kissed your nostril.
Still felt electric.

I wanted to write a poem about love languages.
I thought it could go:

> *He is acts of service,*
> *She is physical touch,*
> *Can I make it any more obvious?!*

To the tune of Avril Lavine's 'Sk8er Boi'. Because, if there's anything I trust to convey emotional nuance, it's early noughties pop-punk.

Then, I got distracted by a forty-seven-minute-long quiz that promised to tell me what my love language is: an untangling of my emotional wiring, via the medium of multiple choice.
Sample question:

> *I feel most loved when my partner*
> *A) Has a meaningful conversation with me*
> *B) Surprises me with something I've been wanting*

Twenty-four minutes in to the forty-seven-minute-long quiz,
I discovered two things:

A) I don't have the patience, and
B) I think my love language is
the arguably simple act of a drunk text.

Drunk Text

I truly believe
there is romance woven between
each and every character of a drunk text.
Love-laden (and booze-fuelled) lassos
looping through the e's,
collecting unsteady vowels and
stringing them together like village fête bunting.

Oh, let your illegible heart sing to mine
from beneath neon stars.
Deliver me tipsy transcriptions in the hours before dawn;
I will thread them on a necklace,
learn your wonky alphabet by heart.
I will devote most of my day
to deciphering the hieroglyphics you sent when
the strobe was your moonlight,
your clavicle shimmering,
weighted head
rolling backward,
fingertips lingering,
somehow
thinking
of me.

There is something in this world that I love even more than a drunk text.

If you can believe such a thing exists.

And that thing, my friends, is absolutely massive knickers.

Big Girl Pants

There comes a time in life when you stop buying arse-floss masquerading as underwear and start shopping for pants like you're in the market for a second-hand hatchback. Is it roomy? you ask yourself. Is it robust? Could you fit a couple of suitcases in the boot?

Now, not to brag, but my knickers[7] are a feat of engineering. Honestly. You could abseil down their seams. Lay them flat and you could host a small picnic on their surface area: a modest charcuterie board, little tub of hummus, maybe even a bottle of cava if you're feeling ambitious.

Once, I fell off a mountain bike, in what witnesses later described as 'a catherine wheel of hairy legs and tragedy'.

It could have ended badly. It *should* have ended badly. But, mid-air, my enormous knickers caught the breeze and deployed themselves into a makeshift parachute.

I gently floated down to safety (not unlike Mary Poppins and her umbrella, drifting past the chimneys of Edwardian London), only slightly scarring a family of hikers and several local dogs in the process.

There's more.

I was trapped at a dinner party, next to a man whose sentences mostly began, *The thing about women is...*

After I had learnt five *things about women*, I asked him to excuse me for just one second. I shimmied under the table, whipped my knickers off and fashioned them into a small tent, where I resided for the remainder of the evening. Aside, of course, from poking a hand out every now and then to pinch a vol-au-vent.

---

7 I'm saying knickers because the word *panties* gives me the ick. Like, sorry, but *panties* was invented by a man who thinks women spend their weekends in matching Victoria's Secret sets, having pillow fights and eating bananas in slow motion.

Another time, in a Las Vegas honky-tonk[8], my How Hard Could It Be gene kicked in as I decided I'd like to ride the mechanical bull. I was wearing a dress, which (unbeknownst to me) is apparently not the done thing, as far as mechanical bulls are concerned. The operator stopped me, frowning. 'No shorts, no ride,' he said, as if quoting scripture.

I hoiked my skirt and flashed him an acre of reinforced cotton. The man gasped, colour draining from his face (poor thing) as he immediately aged ten years. 'You're good,' he croaked, waving me through, both of us knowing he could never unsee what he had seen.

I stayed on that bull for seven days. Missed my flight. Worth every second.

So what's the moral of the story here? Big pants = big life?

Well, yeah.

Big knickers aren't just fabric. They are salvation. They are infrastructure. They get you into and out of places lace, silk and ribbon simply cannot.

And that's the dream, isn't it?

It's not about being the shiniest coin in the wallet, but the one that's been in there so long it's covered in fluff, and also a tiny sticker of a horse for some reason. Do you know what I mean? It's technically legal tender, but everyone's a tiny bit wary about touching it.

I fear I may have let the metaphor get away from me a little bit here. Hang on.

It's not about being the shiniest coin in the wallet, but the most dependable, the one that will undoubtedly be there the next time you need a pound for a trolley.

---

8 Which feels like something you shouldn't be allowed to say, but I've Googled it and I'm pretty sure it's not offensive.

Look, lace is lovely, it's fun, it's flirty, but it's (likely) never saved anyone from a mountain biking disaster. It's never become shelter at a dinner party, never earned you a ride on a mechanical bull.

But big pants have. And, quite frankly, I reckon they always will.

No, in all seriousness, there is something in this world that I love even more than a drunk text and double even more than massive knickers. How d'you like that for a plot twist?

It arrives softly, just sort of walks in and plonks down beside you while you slurp cereal from a mug because all your bowls are dirty. It doesn't request definition or require pageantry; it just shows up without obligation, fanfare or ultimatum again and again and again.

Any guesses yet?

We are told to strive for romance, to search for The One. Conditioned to believe that the romcom soundtrack and the sparkly diamond and the first dance are the pinnacle. Meanwhile, our friends stand on the doorstep, warm Greggs in hand, and there's not a single ounce of judgement when they walk in to find us unkempt, bloated and fourteen episodes into a true crime doc that we only started watching that morning.

Platonic love is not a consolation prize. It's not a wilting side salad; it's the starter, the main course and the post-dinner express martin. I can only speak to my own experience, but it's also far less likely to give you a UTI.

Put it on a T-shirt. A tote bag. A tombstone. One more cocktail and I'm down to tatt it on my lower back. I actually don't really care how we go about it, but I feel very strongly that we should immortalise platonic love.

In Praise of Platonic Love

I don't know much about love.
I don't know much about anything, really,
but I don't think love is grand gestures
like the romcoms we grew up on would have us believe.
I don't think it's meet-cutes
and pebbles at the window
and boomboxes in the rain;
I think it's much simpler than that.

I think love is sleep-drunk bodies
nestled in the crook of a Sunday morning.
McNuggets brought to bedsides
as we dissect the night before.
I think it's raspberry lips fixed in nightclub toilets
and tipsy limbs slipped out of sequins and into softness,
never letting each other drift off in full glam.

I think it's spare hands on unreachable backs,
microfibre mittens laden with fake tan.
It's carefully choreographed dance routines
test-driven in living rooms, then whisked into discos
where we battle with the bassline to scream adoration
inches from each other's sweaty faces.

It's *text me when you get home.*

As our smallest selves,
it's knowing words can wait until tomorrow;
today is for folding our limbs
into each other like origami cranes.
Becoming found fivers tucked into back pockets
for safekeeping,
feeling held enough to break.

It's tampons passed under bathroom stalls
and pep talks on prescription.
Cardigan sleeves wiping tears from bubblegum cheeks,
not brought because the boys don't love us
but because the only frozen fix has been Dulce-de-
Discontinued.

Look, we might not be the movie,
we might not be snogging in the rain
or getting down on one knee
but, really simply,
we're continuing to be the girls of each other's dreams,
the ones we discovered knee-deep in obsessive adolescence,
fell head over jelly heels for
and have held on to, white-knuckled, ever since.

I propose we spend forever falling platonically in love.
I wouldn't trust my foolish heart
in the hands of anyone else anyway.

For nearly twenty-eight years, I've been screaming Spice Girls lyrics to the point where *Wannabe* has become less song, more spiritual mantra. The concept of getting with my friends is now more legal requirement than lyric (take note, prospective lovers), so it's really no great surprise that we should find ourselves here, at the shrine of platonic devotion.

There are certain cultural artefacts from childhood that imprint themselves so deeply into your psyche that they become more than just memories. For me, one such artefact is the VHS of *Spice Girls: Girl Power! Live in Istanbul!*

It is no exaggeration to describe it as a cinematic masterpiece, a cultural relic, featuring the Spice Girls' first ever live performance, interspersed with exclusive interviews and behind-the-scenes footage.

There is one moment. One tiny, throwaway, utterly iconic moment that I have carried with me for years like a precious heirloom. Mel B strides through a hotel corridor, wearing a crop top and snakeskin coat (as one should), and she says with mischievous divinity, 'Don't try this at home, kids, but I've put a diamond in my belly with glue.'

I think about this at least once a week. Couldn't tell you my blood type, but this. This! Is my Roman empire. Ma raison d'être. I couldn't not write it (and her)[9] a poem.

9 Yes, a large portion of this book will just be me writing poems for celebrities I'd like to befriend and/or marry.

Don't Try This at Home, Kids, but I've Put a Diamond in My Belly with Glue

I was small, once. An outline of a girl
close to the telly,
knees pressed together,
body unsure how much space it was allowed to take up.

At the exact same time,
Mel B strides through a hotel corridor,
Don't try this at home, kids,
but I've put a diamond in my belly with glue,
and I'm like, okay,
just bury me under the glittering altar of this moment.

I mean, they probably weren't my exact words,
because I was six,
but I remember thinking
she is electric
in her snakeskin coat,
reptile and royalty all at once,
a girl
and a god
and a lightning bolt.

It makes a home for itself,
this image; its sentiment
puts up a little tent in the hippocampus.[10]

When my science teacher says
girls mature faster than boys like it's a compliment
and not another way to make us mother sooner,
when I wear eyeliner to school and get detention,
when a boy tells me my laugh is not ladylike
and I say cool and laugh again,

10 Had to Google that one, but how fun does it sound?!

I am thinking, the entire time,
of Mel B.
Patron saint of diamonds and defiance
and her belly button,
its shimmering rebellion
skipping to the front of my mind.[11]

So now I wear sequins to brunch,
roll body glitter
onto my collarbones,
onto my best friend's face in the bathroom mirror,
onto the unsmiling cheeks of the security guard
as I ask him if he believes in past lives.

I yell my best friend's name across the street,
let my voice unspool into the night,
make a scene
sticky with sugar and hunger and
the ghosts of girls who taught me how to shine.

I imagine a world where every girl
leaves the house
wearing something she is not supposed to.
Sequins, glue, too much lipstick,
eyelids lined with silver,
rhinestone in her belly button
between a too-short skirt and a too-loud laugh.

Back of her hands stained red
from Superdrug lipstick tests,
drenched in too much perfume.
Heels clicking as she runs for the night bus,
flat-out refusing to be a version of herself
that does not drip with brilliance.

---

11 Or the frontal lobe, if you want to keep it scientific.

Maybe it's ridiculous
to stake a life's work[12] on a throwaway line
from a Spice Girl in a snakeskin coat.
But just in case a six-year-old is watching us,
chewing her sleeve, weighing her worth,
I want her to see sequins and shouting,
gold-foiled girlhood
wrapped in ridiculous, radiant joy,
all of it ours.

12 Dramatic

Objectively Speaking

The getting ready has always been
better than the going out.
A liturgical service of absolute transformation,
it begins when the sun sets
and we gather,
dip the tips of fingers and toes
in lustrous lilac lacquer,
pass frosted bottles between scarlet lips
whilst we mix something else,
something lethal,
something we've nicknamed Death Mix,[13]
take it in turns to take sips
and wait for our vision to blur.

We are doused in devastation,
zipped into something
we picked out the week before
when we emerged from our momentary chrysalis
at the back of the Queensgate New Look
looking more beautiful than we ever could have imagined;
dipped in sequins
and velvet
and 100% polyester,
we are glorious.

Part propped up by heels we can't walk in,
short skirts
and thick gloss
that sticks our lips together when we talk.
I'm wearing five bras,

---

13 Death Mix, if you're interested, is what happens when you're fifteen and committed to poor decisions. To make your own, simply rifle through your parents' drinks cabinet and steal a small splash of every single thing inside: vodka, Baileys, The Green One That Smells Like Toothpaste. Funnel it into a plastic bottle that's been in the bottom of your bag for a week. Shake it. Chug it. Bon appetit.

hoping to create the illusion of tit
(and disguise the fact that underneath
there's nothing but nip)
and, my God, has it worked.

Bright orange,
stinking of biscuits,
which I've tried to disguise by drenching myself
in the scent of Charlie Red.
Skin glistening with perfume and roll-on glitter,
hair crimped,
waists cinched,
Aphrodite's counterparts,
tonight we are
women.

Actual, real, grown-up women.
No, because genuinely, I feel like I could go out now,
come home in the early hours
with a younger man
and a mortgage,
crawl around on my shag pile rug
and say something like
oh, God, I don't know why I drank gin,
I know it makes me weepy.

We boot open the bedroom door,
watch the hairspray haze disperse,
watch it dissolve into nothing
like candyfloss on our tongue,
like the clouds surrounding Mount Olympus,
and from within it, we are birthed.

Call it getting ready,
but know this is ritual,
this is becoming,
our first rite of rebellion,
our inaugural flirt with transgression.

Ode to the Ladies' Loo

This one's for the women whose names I never knew
but befriended somewhere between
the queue and the cubicles.
I think of you often.
It's for the sovereigns of that sacred space
where compliments fly past freshly hairsprayed hair
like paper aeroplanes,
cloistered stories float on whisky-soaked breath,
wisdom is dropped in pockets
as we zip up each other's dresses,
drying tears and wiping sick;
nobody leaves this place a mess.

You can't breathe for adulation,
confidence, praise and admiration.
I mean, I have genuinely left the ladies' loos
the admin of a new WhatsApp group chat,
with a maid of honour
and a promise that someone's firstborn
will be named after me.

This is therapy;
cubicles become confession booths,
drunken shoulders half shrugged off,
damp with mascara.
Glossed lips offering unsolicited love life advice
because, six to a stall and seven gins in,
turns out you're quite philosophical actually.

Between the neon and the nausea
a sisterhood is built in seconds,
like we have never not known each other.
We become hype squads
and poets,

life coaches,
ghostwriters,
photographers
philosophers,
stilettoed saints,
mourners,
mothers,
ex-ex-girlfriends of your mate's cousin's brother.

Here, drunk doesn't mean danger,
and beauty is only reapplied, never reevaluated.
We speak in soft conspiracies,
he was never good enough, anyway,
your eyeliner is an artwork,
and we mean every single word of it.

This is the validation station
where we guarantee you'll leave with twice the vigour
and triple the self-esteem,
but not before
you're ushered into a photoshoot in the corner:
like, full production,
the hand dryer is our makeshift wind machine,
and we'll wake up to
might as well be double-page spreads,
blurry photos, banging heads,
a gallery of girls we can't remember,
the ones we loved in the half-light,
half-cut, wholehearted,
the ones we are so, so glad we met.

The gorgeous little ecosystem of the nightclub toilet exists in stark contrast to the hours that precede it.

In the prologue, in our uniform (varying versions of Jeans And A Nice Top), we sit cross-legged in front of the mirror, heads stacked atop each other like a totem pole. We curl and spritz and pout, and then we all join in for a chorus of soft-spoken self-deprecation, listing our flaws as if we're about to auction them off.

It's like that scene in *Mean Girls* where they stand in Regina's pink bedroom, zooming in on their micro-flaws:
My hairline is so weird.
My pores are huge.
My nail beds suck.

I'm not above this ritual. In fact, it's a favourite pastime of mine (alongside devouring 'sharing' bags of crisps and adding items to my online basket, but never ever proceeding to checkout).

But there is a particular kind of heartbreak in watching people you love slowly convince themselves they are subpar. I mean, these are people I would throw myself into traffic for, and they are debating not going out tonight because, at certain angles, their knees look like an old man's face.

So this next one is for anyone who has ever stood in front of a mirror and forgotten, if only for a moment, how lovely they are.

Size 8

I hope you know
we're only friends because you're a size 8.
You know that, right?
Because I have standards
and you have symmetry
and that's why this works.

Not tryna be rude, just keen to clarify.

I like you only because
your body nips in at the middle,
turning your corporeal form cursive.
I like your hip-to-waist ratio, mate,
and more than that, I like the fact
your hair is thick
and your skin is clear
and because if, by some strange miracle,
I shrank down to an inch and a half tall,
I could ski off the cute little piste of your nose.

I like that there is no cellulite
and that your head fits four, not three or five.
I like that there are no bingo wings
or wobbly things.
I am so grateful you've had braces,
because if you hadn't
I don't know that we'd be here, now,
having this conversation.

Okay, so doesn't it sound ridiculous
when I say it?

When I think about you,
it's never your thighs

or your arms
or your belly
or your calves.
I'm not here for your cheekbones
or the width of your waist,
but for the days we feel shaped like nothing at all
and still find ourselves held in place
by each other.

Side by side,
picking the lint off each other's bad days.
I'm in for the way we both show up
with all of our wish-this-was-differents,
plonk ourselves down
like two coats on the backs of chairs.
Four unfinished thoughts and three drinks in,
we don't flinch
at each other's ugly cries;
we order another bowl of chips
and snort-laugh until a nearby table complains.

I like the nights we set the world to rights
without solving a single thing.
I like your dance moves
and your Paul Hollywood impression
and, even though I am thirty and perfectly capable
of regulating my own body temperature,
I like the way you still ask if I'm taking a coat.

Of course I think you're beautiful,
but I'm not just measuring aesthetically.
I would love you if your body was shaped like a Curly Wurly;
you know that.

You are beautiful because of all of the above,
and then some.
So, if I love you like this,
never once equating worth with hip dips
or smooth skin,
just fully, stupidly, without condition,
listen, not tryna tell you what to do,
but I reckon you should love yourself that way too.

If loving yourself still sometimes feels like trying to apply mascara in a moving vehicle, I've got a life hack for you.

It's unofficially sponsored by this wonderfully trashy crime/thriller novel I've been reading, in which the author spends more time describing the female characters' breasts than he does advancing the plot.

Still, magic lives in unlikely places, so, should you ever feel like a literal stale heel of bread, give this a go. Let me know how it works out.

Are We Admiring Our Breasts, Then, or What?

On the days you feel less than,
which, by the way,
I hope are few and far between,
I'd like to invite you to admire your breasts
as if they have been written
by a sixty-something-year-old man,
penning his debut
crime thriller/sexy romp novel
in the summerhouse at the bottom of his garden.

Carve out time to admire their size,
their previously undiscovered sentience.
You've likely never lingered
on their ability to be startled
or appreciative.
Linger a while,
cocoon yourself in the comforting embrace
of misogyny disguised as literature.

On the days you feel less than,
which, by the way, I hope are few and far between,
do not set off in pursuit of purpose and worth.
Your value lies solely in the heft of your bosom;
you know that.
The way it heaves with convenience,
sways with the faintest shake of a head.
You've likely never appreciated
the way your breasts
could hypothetically suss out a serial killer
just a couple of seconds before your brain does.
Or, perhaps,
the way they roll,
in perfect sync with your eyes.

On the days you feel less than,
which, by now it should go without saying,
I hope are few and far between,
it is only fair to assume
the majesty that exists in your mammaries
must flow through you in your entirety,
bubble in the very marrow of your bones,
trickle from soft lips
as you whisper and WhatsApp incantations,
trace trees back generations,
learn you are stitched into the bloodline of witches,
magic leaking
from every inch of you.

If that doesn't work, maybe you're hungry. Or dehydrated.

Maybe you're in your luteal phase.[14] Maybe you have neither breasts nor a luteal phase, in which case I hope you haven't been feeling excluded.

Maybe you're tired, or tangled, or a little bit frayed at the edges. Maybe we're all just Having A Bit Of A Time.

That's alright.

Feelings have corners and sometimes, like a Sim unable to walk through an unobstructed doorway, we get stuck in them. In any case, much like bad hangovers or karaoke-booth birthday parties, this too shall pass. Promise.

14 You poor thing.

Bad Day

Let the world happen without me.
I want to lie in bed,
drift in and out of consciousness,
watch the first and third quarters of a film.
Suck Wotsit dust from my fingertips. I want
to be immovable
(unless I truly, desperately need a wee).
I want to be ugly,
not the kind you can sell in the cinema,
oversized T-shirt and messy bun,
sobbing clean lines
down cheeks still soft enough to kiss.
I want my roots to worm deep into the mattress,
rupturing foam and coil.
I want to harden like a peach stone,
stay firm in the unripened flesh,
more fossil than fruit.

Yesterday, I was a cloud,
but now, seemingly without reason,
I am a threadbare thing
snagging on tarmac.
Hate to break it to you, Daniel Powter, my love,
but sometimes, on the really bad ones,
when the sun is crooked
and my limbs are overcooked pasta,
singing a sad song just isn't gonna cut it.
On those days, it is all I can do
to surrender my sagging body
to the mouth of the sofa,
order enough takeaway to feed a family of five
and try again tomorrow.

Chia Pudding

Sorry, I've literally just made chia pudding.
Not literally. About two hours ago, but still.
Smug about it.
Texted a friend about it.
Telling you about it.
(I mean, yeah, it's literally just chia seeds and milk,
but you've gotta celebrate the little wins where you can.)

I washed the bowl I made the pudding in,
and have spent about seventeen minutes (so far) plucking
those slippery little frogspawny bastards
from my microfibre cloth.
My worry is the seeds will otherwise
slip down the plughole, like a rubber ring
in a water park, acquiescing to
the undulations of the slide.
I'm worried if I don't get them all,
I'll end up like that guy who
accidentally flooded his neighbourhood with Orbeez.[15]

While we're on the subject,[16]
I'm worried
I should've made more of the day's infrequent sunshine
instead of marinating in emails
and instant coffee.
Was it a mistake

---

15 Have you seen this? It's an absolute masterclass in poor decision making. A French influencer fills his bathtub with Orbeez water beads, and you're watching like, okay, cool, quirky bath vid. When he pulls the plug out, the Orbeez clog the entire system. Desperately trying to get rid, he flushes the toilet, but the pipes are blocked and the toilet water floods his bathroom. It gets worse and worse until the end of the video, where the entire neighbourhood's sewage system has been blocked by Orbeez, they're popping out of the drains in the street and the mayor(!!) is looking for the culprit..

16 Of worry, not Orbeez.

to skip the pink streaks of sunset
in favour of font deliberation?
Was it a waste
to weigh pros and cons of Helvetica Neue?
Is that a good use
of my one wild and precious life?

Okay, so, like, in for a penny:
I'm worried about the future
and the lingering instability of
Words As A Career.
I'm worried I've given too many hours
to my laptop this year,
not nearly enough
to beer gardens
and factor 50
and inelegant pirouettes
through the no man's land between the back
of the sofa and the washing machine.

I'm worried all my poems sound the same,
which is basically just like,
slow down,
eat pizza for breakfast,
nobody knows what they're doing,
everything will be alright.

I'm worried that pizza for breakfast
probably isn't the best advice.

I'm worried that I'm living for the now
but forgetting to moisturise for the future,
which is to say
I don't know how to build a life for later
while making the most of the one
I have this week.

I'm worried that I'm moving too slowly
and all my friends are spreading out.
I'm worried that I can name
more of the cast of *Geordie Shore*
than I can endangered species
and my reusable water bottle
is basically just a prop.
I'm worried my poor posture might be irreversible
because I physically can't not sit like a croissant.
I'm worried my nipples
might be larger than average
and I'm eating too many crisps,
washing my hair too often
and my shower door too little,
and that the last full book I read was a menu
and even then, I skimmed it.

But the thing is,
when you think about it,
worrier and *warrior* are only a couple of letters apart,
and, while that sounds like something you'd find
stitched into an embroidery hoop
in your therapist's waiting room
or unfolding from your yoga teacher's mouth
before she charges £90 for a cacao ceremony
(not naming names, Heather),
maybe it's also not the worst thing ever.

Maybe it's okay
if I don't save the whales by Tuesday.
I can learn what kind of whales we're talking about.
I can call my mum while I'm cooking pasta;
I can let a few chia seeds slip down.
I can reply to the group chat,
remember to bring my own bag to the shop.
Tiny shifts.

Bit by bit.
And, in the meantime,
slow down,
eat pizza for breakfast,
nobody knows what they're doing,
everything will be alright.

Burger Nips

As you know (unless you've skipped ahead (you big naughty)), I have a strong suspicion my nipples are, to use a medical term, absolutely massive.

Not the little *cherry-on-top* bit. Not the cute little *OMG-is-there-a-draught-in-this-artisanal-brunch-spot* bit, the bit that charmingly salutes strangers whenever the temperature drops below eight degrees. I'm talking about the surrounding postcodes. The welcome mat. The Areola Grandes, if you will.

Have I seen enough other nipples to verify this?
Absolutely not.
Would I like to see more nipples?
Yes. For science (of course), and also for morale.

But I just can't find a way in, I mean, it's not the sort of thing you can bring up on your lunch break, leaning over a Pret salad like 'how's the Anders presentation looking, and also, just quickly, what's the diameter of your nipple?'

Occasionally, I might catch a glimpse on the beach, a rogue topless sunbather (God bless her) suggesting what the standard issue might look like. Beyond that, I haven't got a scoob. I have absolutely not conducted sufficient research to confirm or deny my suspicions.

I have, however, dreamt about the existence of an underground, high-stakes nipple comparison ring. You slip through a velvet curtain into a smoky back room, where you flash your chebs to a big bald man with a clipboard and a tiny woman with a razor-sharp micro-fringe. They look at you. No words. Just a solemn nod or a gentle, pitying shake of the head. Then you zip up your hoodie, dignity slightly askew, and melt back into the night.

Let's say such a place existed, let's say I had a solid grasp of the National Nipple Averages, what then? Am I going to write a thesis? Doubtful. So what would be the point? To arm myself with a new insecurity? Turn a harmless observation into another private neurosis I can nurture for years like a sickly houseplant?

Things is, when all is said and done, whether I'm looking left, right, or straight down the barrel of an OnlyFans account, my nips are staying exactly as they are. You can spend your whole life studying other people's nipples, but you've still gotta live inside your own T-shirt. The only thing that shrinks when you compare is your peace of mind.

Body

Oh, what it would be like
to not be at war with yourself
every time the sun comes out.

Virgin Active, Cricklewood

I've got a confession to make.

I've been looking at the women
in the changing rooms at the gym.

I know how that sounds,
but I just want to be really clear about one thing:
I was not using the gym.
My flatmate works on the front desk
and sneaks me in to have a little sit in the steam room and/or sauna.

On this occasion, I'm getting ready for a swim,
hoping nobody looks at me.
I'm wondering if there's a way I can get my costume on
without taking off my jeans
(God forbid anybody sees what I've got hiding underneath).

I'm mid-manoeuvre
and it's gone a bit wrong;
my full-coverage costume has turned into a thong,
down below I've got two legs in the same hole,
and up here my old bracelet has snagged
on my new chunky knit.
Then, before I can snatch it,
my costume starts to slip,
so I fall forward,
elastic pings,
knickers and bras fall to the floor, with my jeans,
and before I know it
I am almost completely naked,
totally exposed
and awkwardly sprawled on the floor
of the women's changing rooms at Virgin Active,

Cricklewood branch,
and
nobody notices.
Nobody gives a shit.
Nobody sees my naked body
and is immediately sick;
they're too busy
towel-drying freshly showered skin,
distracted by nail varnish that's worn too thin,
yanking tights over not-quite-dry thighs.
There's one woman
in the corner, with her leg up on a chair,
just full-on hairdrying her pubes.

I can't remember the last time I saw women like this.

Post-work,
post-workout women.
Out of breath,
hair glued down to sweating heads,
post-gym,
post-swim women.
Rolling bikini bottoms over cellulite
and wobbling thighs.
I can't remember the last time I saw women like this.
Real women.
And I don't mean *Dove Campaign* 'Real Women' real women;
I mean actual real women.

Women with stretch marks from ankle to thigh,
with curved bellies
and tired eyes.
Women with leg hair and armpit hair;
there are thousands of pubes
and lopsided boobs,
there are lean thighs that don't touch

and then thighs that do,
there are six-packs and sculpted backs,
slender arms and rolls of fat,
there is acne and bacne and wobbling bums
and birthmarks and scars
and post-school-run mums
wrangling hordes of goggle-eyed children
towards the pool
and of course I am shocked.

Not because of anything these women have
or haven't got
but because I can't believe
I've never seen this before.
I have never seen so much normal.
Instead I've been fed these billboard-sized
bright-eyed, white-toothed women
who pose, scantily clad
as parenthetical limbs frame slender finger
on slender waist,
insurmountably symmetrical.
Photoshopped and filtered
within an inch of their lives,
so much so you couldn't pick the original woman
out of a line-up.
This, comparatively, feels like
a glorious magic lair.

On the way home,
I want to scream in the face of every woman I pass
that we should all just *stop caring!*
I want to bottle this,
give one to every woman I know and tell her to
have a little bit if she's feeling crap
or, failing that,
get herself down to Virgin Active,

Cricklewood branch.
That's where the real women are,
fierce and enchanting,
wriggling out of sports bras
whilst sweat ferries mascara into their dark circles.

This feels like a real
moment.
One I will inevitably, momentarily forget
the next time I see a gorgeous stranger in a bikini
and think
I wanna look like that.
But for now,
whilst it's here, whilst I've got it,
I feel like celebrating.

Love Language

So I finished the quiz.

D'you remember the What's Your Love Language quiz I was telling you about earlier? Honestly, nothing says *looming literary deadline* like returning to twenty-three minutes of unanswered, unnecessary personality testing.

Anyway, turns out my love language isn't drunk texts (but maybe only because they're not one of the options); turns out my love language is gifts.

Gifts! How genuinely devastating.

You'd want it to be quality time or words of affirmation or one of the ones that make you look like a good, emotionally mature, selfless person. But I guess I just love stuff. I'm a magpie, basically, in dungarees and an oversized cardigan.

In fairness, the online personality quiz gods are not wrong. Nothing turns me on quite as much as spending six hours alone at TK Maxx, filling my basket with ceramic plates shaped like tropical fruits.

In the past six months, I've purchased three platters so large, they may actually be portals to another dimension. They sit somewhere between kitsch and objectively repulsive and I'm head over heels. They also literally sit on the kitchen counter, because they do not fit in any cupboard, but I will never get rid of them because they are gorgeous and unnecessary and remind me that love (much like sizeable ceramics) is sometimes wildly impractical.

Oh, speaking of sizeable things, Google Peter Glazebrook before you read the next one.

Reading that sentence back, it doesn't sound good. Or at least it doesn't sound PG. I'll admit that.

I'm not trying to embarrass you in public (or wherever you're reading this); it's honestly not what you think. And by *what you think*, I mean it's not what I've explicitly made it sound like.

Not Shallot to Ask For

All I really long for in this life
is to be looked at
the way Peter Glazebrook looks
at his award-winning onion.

Mr Whippy, Why Not

One of my top-tier,
ten-out-of-ten,
would absolutely, without question recommend to a friend,
five-star-Tripadvisor-rated
things to experience is –
sorry,
I need to make sure you understand
just how much I love this;
I'm talking, like, up there with
fresh bedsheets
and cancelling plans,
as good as the cold side of the pillow
or, after months of darkness,
the first breath of spring,
like, put this on a plinth
in my private Museum of Perfect Things –
all I ever want to witness is

a businessman,
mid-forties, mid-fifties,
sensible shoes,
in a full-grown, full-blown suit,
waddling around in broad daylight
absolutely hoofing a Mr Whippy.

There is no greater vibe.
No higher art form.
He's just a man, who is still a boy,
being told that we're not going to do double geography after lunch;
the sun's out, so we'll stay on the field
and play rounders.

Double Flake? Absolutely.
Triple, if you've got it, good sir.
This is not
I did a bad merger and now I need to heal;
this is the purest cultivation of joy.

He's out here, collar unbuttoned,
loosening himself from the day
like a petal peeling back from its flower.
Trousers lightly seasoned with ice cream drips,
tie flapping like a windsock,
raspberry sauce baptising his wrists
and he doesn't wipe it away.

He stands there, sticky and slow.
The ice cream van singing
its tinny little ding dong song,
and for one glorious moment
neither of us can remember
why we ever thought we had to grow up.

Brunch

At brunch, my friends talk about soft play areas and meal planning. I don't know what soft play is.

It sounds like a euphemism for something unspeakable. Like something I'd tell you to Google under the guise of poetic context.

Either that or an experimental theatre company.

My friends exchange tips on how to hide vegetables in pasta sauce and compare BPA-free weaning spoons. I nod along, swirling my mimosa, as if I, too, have spent my morning blending courgettes into a stealthy purée rather than trying to decipher whether Tom Holland and Zendaya are still together based on subtle Instagram activity.

I saw a fox eat an entire sausage roll last night, I say, hoping to shift the energy towards my own interests: urban wildlife and carbohydrates.

They blink at me like I'm a push notification. One of them attaches a baby to her boob. That's nice, she says, in the same tone you might use to reply to an elderly relative recounting a dream about a talking dolphin. *That's nice, Uncle Albert; very helpful of the dolphin to give you directions, isn't it?*

After brunch, I spend £5 on a coffee I don't really want. I just need an activity. I need to feel like I belong somewhere. I walk home thinking about the past.

On the common, I remember how we'd all end up in someone's bed, eating crisps at 2am, drunk and heartbroken over men who wear boat shoes without socks and shag with their AirPods in.

I think about the matching and inevitably infected belly button piercings we got in an act of sisterhood, despite none of us ever having shown an inch of midriff.

Now, even catching up feels fragile. Like somehow describing my life feels like a quiet betrayal of theirs. I find myself editing out details, and I hate it. I don't know when the ground exclusively became thin ice and eggshells, but I'm reluctant to take a single step, in fear of the cracks that might appear. I'm afraid that every word out of my mouth might accidentally expose the gap that has opened between us.

So we just keep walking alongside each other, our lives running parallel, still close enough to ask how work is or go halves on an almond croissant, but the girls who once upon a time believed they were indestructible, the girls who thought they could survive anything, so long as they held on tight enough, are gone. And none of us are brave enough to say it.

Reason, Season, Lifetime

We bought nectarines from the farmer's market,
let their juice dribble down our chins,
bare legs on the common at the first sign of spring.
Then red wine winters,
where we'd get in the same bed
just to warm it up and stay until morning.

You somersaulted into something wonderful,
and he is gentle,
wraps his arms around you in public, like
he knows he's caught a rare thing.
The type of love we lit candles and burned sage for
when we were drunk at 2am
waiting for fried chicken to arrive.

I used to know where your inhaler was,
what you were having for dinner,
when to put the period playlist on.
I was agony aunt,
wardrobe extension,
and now I am a story you might tell
when he asks about your past.

I thought you were every season,
the frost, the thaw, the full, brilliant bloom;
I thought you were the lifetime.
But maybe you were the reason,
existing to teach me what true love looks like.

Anyway, I've put the nectarines and the sage
and the twenty-seven minutes we waited for fried chicken
in that gingham pouch you once used for tampons,
in case you want them

for your something borrowed. Although
I think I was the one who was borrowing.

God,
wasn't it brilliant
while it lasted?

How to Decide Things

At the pub,
my friend tells me she's pregnant.
I say congratulations, with my whole face
and my whole heart,
and then I awkwardly wrap my arms around her
and try not to touch her with my hands
still sticky from spilling my drink.

How do people just decide things?

How do they have conversations about
leaving contraceptives in the drawer,
or the packet?
How do they know now is the time
to grow tiny soft humans
who giggle and cry and paint macaroni with gold glitter?

Last week, I spent two hours trying to decide
whether I should or should not buy
a wood wick candle.
Two hours. One candle.[17]
Two hours of weighing up cedar versus sandal,
and in the end I decided against it.

All I really know
is the way I hold my own life
like a soft peach,
turning it over in my hands,
checking for bruises.

And I do also know
that some people have life plans,

---

17 Sorry, but can you ever say *two something one something* without thinking about 2 Girls 1 Cup? Where are they now, I wonder.

and some people Google things like
what happens to your microbiome
if you eat hummus for every meal,[18]
and maybe that's fine.
Maybe it's perfect.
Maybe life is just one big, gorgeous, terrifying buffet,
where some people beeline for the roast beef
and some people fill their plates with crisps and pâté
or just keep drinking prosecco by the bread section.
So I tell her congratulations again,
because what I mean is I love
that you are sure,
and I love that I am not.

18 Hypothetically.

You Don't Have to If You Don't Want To / A Soft Rebellion

Let them go.
Let them go, with their rush-hour lives.
Not everyone has to rise at dawn
and do hot yoga.
It is not compulsory to chug a lemon water
and find your purpose before 7am.
Not every morning has to be peeled
and cut into clean slices.
The mornings can stay whole,
unbroken,
a thing you pick up
and put down again.

You don't need to dress for company;
you can stay soft,
watch the slant of light crawl
across your carpet,
eat toast so thick with butter
you leave teeth marks,
wear the same bra seventeen days in a row.

I suppose what I'm saying is
you're allowed to do things differently,
to pause, if you need to,
to be a Sunday even on a Tuesday.

And when they come,
all wide-eyed and puzzled,
asking how you've done it,
shrug.
Tell them you haven't, really.

The secret
is that there is no secret.
You just stopped moving like the rest of them,
and the world spun[19] anyway.

19 Is it SO unsatisfying that the book title is *spins* and this is *spun*? The deliberations over spins/spun/spone were mighty. This needed to be past tense, because you've already made the decision, but having the title in the past tense made me feel like the world had stopped spinning and ended. So, look, it is what it is.

I'm learning to trust the pause. I'm learning that growth doesn't always look like movement and some days, the best thing you can do for yourself is nothing at all. But also, what is life without a little drama, mama?

So I've made a list.

I wrote it in January, but they're not resolutions, because I'm not a lover of resolutions. I don't really like their vibe:

- lose a stone
- learn to love kale
- stop wasting money on candles that smell like the memory of a storm

They feel punitive, y'know?
Like you're setting yourself up to fail.

I've decided I prefer intentions. They're softer, more forgiving, not really bothered whether you succeed or don't. Intentions just want you to 'ave a little go, babes. So let's 'ave a little go, babes.

Twenty-Five for '25

1. More dramatic exits.

2. More dramatic kissing.
   Ideally, end of the world style.
   Pressed against a cold wall
   in the dim glow of emergency lights,
   like this might be
   The Last Kiss Before The Universe Unravels.
   The last kiss before aliens break the door down,
   the kind of kissing
   that makes your heart pound
   like it's just remembered what it's for.

3. Commit to a dramatic hobby, like archery or blues harmonica.

4. Say no more.
   'Scuse me, say *no* more.
   Unless the question is *would madame*
   care for another canapé?

5. Eat more canapés.

6. Up the Main Character Energy.
   More pretending I'm in Paris
   when actually
   I'm on the 08.13 to Elephant and Castle.
   Sigh-whisper *Je suis fatigué*
   to no one in particular.

7. Don't be afraid to look ridiculous. It's better than being afraid to try.

8. Rewatch *Mamma Mia!* once a month to remind myself

what true art looks like.

9. Finish a book before buying three more.

10. Say yes to last-minute plans.

11. As often as possible, feel more Fergalicious.

12. Be astonished by something small every day: a shadow, a sentence, a spoon.

13. Learn to make an excellent martini.

14. Learn to drink a martini excellently.
    Which is to say
    without asking ten people
    whether they hate my fringe or not
    and then locking myself in the bathroom.

15. Dress like I have my shit together even when I'm crying into a Pret sandwich.

16. Stop buying Pret sandwiches.
    £6.25 is too much
    for an inch of avocado and three olives.

17. Tell the people I love that I love them way more often.

18. Own fewer mugs.[20]

19. At least once this year, shout *you'll regret this when I'm famous!*
    Leave the room.
    Refuse to clarify.
    See point number one.

---

20 I shared this poem online and got a *lot* of heat for this one. I stand by it.

20. Dress up without occasion.

21. Be a little bit softer.

22. Be a little bit louder.

23. Forgive often.

24. Don't worry about making sense of it all. Just keep dancing.

25. Remember that the most interesting, kind, hilarious, supportive, wonderful people I know are still figuring it out too.

Better Than Being Afraid to Try

We are alive and we are trying.
Like three raccoons, stacked in a trench coat,
pretending to be a person.

Yesterday, a stranger smiled at me,
and I swear the whole city exhaled.
I think, sometimes,
trying means ordering the £19 carbonara
and calling it self-care.
I think it also means not hating yourself
for texting *you up?* at 3am,
or pressing send on essays
that should have never left the notes app.
You can't know until you know,
you know?

I think trying looks like apologising too much,
then not enough,
like saying *yeah, fine, thanks* when actually
you are one tiny gust of wind away
from hysterically crying at the bus stop.

It's the space between what you wanted
and what it is.
Asking questions
and asking for help
and watering the plant
even though the leaves
have already filed for emancipation
because you believe in revival.

We are alive and we are trying
and that is enough.

That is the whole thing, actually.

Queen of Second Chances

I am trying to practise self-love,
but I keep getting distracted
and falling in love with DJs
or comedians
or (worse) men who want to be DJs or comedians
or (even worse) a man who described himself as
vaguely ambient.[21]

When the men show up, late,
I tell them it's okay;
I brought a book with me, anyway.
Then, after the date, after eight to ten working days,
when they eventually reply,
I tell them it's fine.
When they disappear completely,
I turn inward,
assume the fault is mine.

I've started handing out loyalty cards
stamped with hot foil
(even my delusion has standards):
ask for 9 absolutions, get the 10th for free,
hoping that means there's something
to stick around for.

I have built a church inside my own chest,
nothing fancy;
it leaks when it rains
and the hymn sheets have seen better days,
but I've spread the loyalty cards on the altar,
so when the men shuffle in,
apologies loose and half-forgotten,

21 What even is that? How do you describe yourself as vaguely ambient and keep a straight face?

uh, my bad, work's been crazy lately,
or
I had a dream about you and the vibes were really confusing,
or
I got super into fermenting my own kefir and forgot to message,
I can stamp, stamp, stamp.
The second their lips petition forgiveness
I become the Oprah of exoneration:
you get a stamp! You get a stamp! You get a stamp!
Crack open my ribcage, candles already burning,
and let them back in.

Hopefully, one day,
someone will exist
who doesn't need ten chances
to get it right the first time.

Subtraction

I'm trying to cradle myself through heartbreak,
to hold my own hand, as if it's
not attached to the same body
that keeps breaking open.

On the bus, I watch a couple share headphones,
heads close enough
to catch the same breath, and I wonder
if they know the risk they're taking,
letting someone else's song into their soundtrack.

I can't stop refreshing Instagram
to see if he's posted,
to see – what? If he's still alive,
if his dimples are still there,
still deep enough to drown in.

That's the thing about heartbreak:
one day you're a rational human being,
then suddenly
you are an unhinged woman
in a dressing gown
stained with over-dunked biscuits,
refreshing Instagram
to see if they still like Jungle
or, worse,
if they like someone else.

How can you begin to make sense of the fact that
the person who once made you feel full
is now the reason you feel hollow?

Healing is not glamorous,
it is dishevelled and undignified and unkind,
but it is also
almost always
just a matter of time.
It is learning to master
the slow art of subtraction,
where you keep
taking away
and
take
ing
a
way
until
finally
you add up to yourself again.

Bathing when you're heartbroken is one of life's great pleasures. It's up there with watching businessmen enjoy a Mr Whippy.

Well, not quite. That's top-tier, as we've discussed. I s'pose it's more akin to finding a fiver in an old coat pocket, or eavesdropping by the pool on holiday.

Normally, baths are off the table for me. They make me feel like a boiled gammon. Y'know, the bit before the roasting, when you chuck it in a saucepan with a handful of peppercorns and a bay leaf for an hour or so.

Coupled with the brightness, it's just absolutely not happening. I mean, who decided most bathrooms should be devoid of mood lighting? I want to feel mysterious and aloof in there, not like I'm about to get embalmed.

Honestly, the thought of my nudey, pink, vulnerable bod being lit like Javert at the barricade for a sell-out Saturday matinée is just not the one. I demand a dimmer switch.

However, the exception to the ~~rule~~ feeling is the days my heart has been torn asunder. On those days, I'll light seventy-three candles and lower myself through the bubbles like a little naked mole rat on a wellness retreat.

Fatter in the Bath

I have poured half a bottle of Burt's Bees Tub Time bubbles
into the bath,
which, for future reference, is too much.
My self-care knows no bounds.

I am fatter in the bath.
I don't know the science, I'm not Albert Einstein,
but only in the bath
does my belly become dropped ribbon
rippling like a Viennetta,
each swell
a momentary emergence from foam
like the infamous protuberances of the Loch Ness monster.

It's quite nice.
The soft fistfuls of flesh that sit just above my hips
existing, unfiltered, in this privacy.
The stretch marks on my thighs
are neither tiger stripes nor lightning bolts
but a postcard from the past,
a memory of the body I outgrew.

Every roll, every scar, every dimple
a glorious corporeal decoration,
a small chapter in the story
of how I got to be exactly where I am.

Skin has texture,
delicate etchings and deep lines
at the corners of eyes
drawn slowly over years of squinting into joy.
The echoes of laughter
reappearing with every smile,
a reminder that consistent happiness
will not leave you unblemished.

I have grown
and tightened
and stretched
and shrunk.
I have struggled
and survived
and overcome.
I have lived laughed loved
and I get to wear the proof on my skin.

If you're sat in the bath,
grappling with a body that has carried you
through this world,
I hope you learn to love the evidence.

A Contradiction

When I am washing the dishes I am holding in my stomach,
squeezing suds from the sponge and wishing
I could wring inches from my thighs like water from the dishcloth,
twist the fat from bone,
my hands slick with soap and self-loathing.

I am not proud of this,
but I am also not surprised.
It is a slow education, this vanishing act,
the way a girl learns to shrink before she learns to grow.

Seeds were sown between the pages of *Heat* magazine,
where Britney's body became public property
and Lindsay's weight was up for debate.
We were raised by the Circle of Shame,
where someone in an office
got to slap a red circle on celebrity cellulite
and call it journalism.
Where actual boardrooms decided
that a woman eating a burger was news.
I imagine them scurrying into their glass-walled office
like ants into the colony,
A celebrity has gained weight!
Cancel everything!
We must all discuss it!

They taught us young
that our bodies are everyone's business except our own.
In the dim glow of MSN Messenger,
we learnt to type *ugh, I look disgusting*
before anyone else could beat us to the punchline.

By the time we were grown, it was instinct.

A twitch in the fingers, a reflex in the gut.
They raised us like this,
gave us entire industries designed
to make us feel unworthy,
told us we were broken,
then sold us the glue.

And yeah, I know.
I *knowww-uh.*
I am meant to be better than this by now,
meant to have chucked all that shame in the bin
along with the diet teas and the push-up bras,
but some things sit too deep in the skin.
There are still moments of hesitation,
when I see a picture of myself and wonder
not *do I look happy?* but *do I look thin?*
Echoes of the lessons we never asked to learn.

Even now, when I sit in a bikini,
I don't actually sit.
I arrange.

A man I once loved never took his T-shirt off at the beach.
He said it was because he burned easily,
but I always suspected he felt exactly like I did,
like taking up space was a crime
and showing skin was an offence.
And now, when I stand there,
hands clutching the hem of my T-shirt,
I think about him,
and about all the people sitting on their towels,
holding their breath,
waiting for someone else to go first.

Return of the Low-Rise Jean

There are some things we, as a society,
have collectively agreed to move past:
dial-up internet,
jeggings,
writing 'cryptic' MSN statuses like
~~*sometimes goodbye is a second chance*~~ (wilting rose emoji).

We buried them deep, patted the soil
and made a solemn four-syllable vow:
never again.[22]
But here we are;
the low-rise jean has risen
from the ashes of our trauma
like a Y2K zombie in a Von Dutch trucker hat.
It started innocuously enough,
a whisper in the wind,
a shadow at the edges of an ASOS *checking us out, huh* email.
Then Bella Hadid wore a pair.
Then Emily Ratajkowski.
And now, like the girl in a horror movie
realising the call is coming from inside the house,
I'm standing in a Zara changing room,
clutching a denim belt loop, crying.

How has it come to this?

---

22 Are you counting the syllables? It is four, I promise.

You know what's even more traumatic than low-rise jeans? And I say this as someone who once broke a sweat (and a seam) trying to wedge myself into a pair so tight I briefly lost circulation in my left leg. Though the truest shame was when the button popped off and hit the mirror, so then I had to buy the bastard things.

But d'you know what's even worse?

Being called a girlboss.

I was recently called a girlboss by someone carrying a keep cup that said *CEO OF MYSELF* in looping gold letters. I had to go for a lie down.

Listen, I love feminism. I love buying things I don't need to fill the aching void. I exist slap bang in the middle of this weird little Venn diagram. But even for me, it's all getting a bit much.

This is feminism without action, feminism as merch, where the empowerment lives in the font, not the fight.

I honestly wouldn't even flinch if the next tampon I used had *smash the patriarchy* crocheted into the string.

If I Am Ever Called a Girlboss

please know it is against my will.

Please know that I was mid-sentence,
talking about something inconsequential,
something so small
it became the only thing that really mattered;
you know the way that happens?
Like how my nanna only ever drank sparkling water,
or the smell of sun-warmed pavements in August.
I was talking about something soft
when *girlboss*, sharp as a bitten lip,
was placed in my mouth,
its vowels already chewed.
Listen, I don't wanna be rude, but
I was never built for power blazers,
for glossy coworking spaces
with neon signs that say *slay every day,*
as if the key to ambition is a catchphrase.
I was never meant to stand on stage with a head mic
and gesture to a PowerPoint slide that says
don't be a lady, be a legend.

Why must women's ambition always be wrapped in wordplay,
softened with a joke,
with a curated aesthetic so no one feels threatened?
Our success sold back to us,
souvenirs from the battle we have not finished fighting;
nothing says revolution quite like
a keyring and a matching T-shirt,
glittering pin badges and canvas tote bags,
as if we wouldn't know how to want things
without being reminded by iridescent lettering.

I could be wrong,
but I don't reckon the suffragettes chained themselves to railings,
flung their bodies beneath galloping hooves
in the hope that one day, women of the future
might hang a cursive print
she believed she could, so she did
in their kitchens.[23]

I don't want a smaller version of success with frilled edges,
built like a patronising pat on the head.
When men succeed they are just successful;
there is no *boy* boss,
there is no branded water bottle
reminding him to *hydrate and hustle*,
there is no dinky little suffix stuck to the front.
Girl is a word they use
to make power seem cute,
less threatening,
more digestible;
the more bite-sized you make us,
the less likely we are to get stuck in your throat.

---

23 No offence if you have that, by the way.

I met a friend for a drink recently, and I was telling her about this book. As in, this very book you're holding in your hands.

And she goes *yeah, but what do you want to do with your life?*

There was a sassy little tilt on the *do*, like everything I'm *doing* now (the writing, the wobbling, the bingeing *Below Deck: Mediterranean* while eating cold leftovers at three o'clock on a Wednesday) doesn't really count.

It's strange, isn't it, the way people talk about doing, like it's the most important verb?

People like to measure worth by output, so they ask questions like *what do you do*, and secretly they mean *what are you worth*, the little sneakies! Creativity gets folded up and filed under *hobby* unless it's accompanied by prestige. Like, you're only an actor if you've been in a film they've seen. You're only an artist if your painting has hung beside a small plaque in a cold room. Your current existence is a warm-up for when you really start Doing Stuff. Stuff that presumably requires a LinkedIn profile and a pension scheme.

And all I can think is *what a sad little life, Jane.*

We've become so obsessed with doing, we've forgotten about

being, and being, surely, is the whole point.

There's no single template, no right way to exist. On the quiet days, in the 'unproductive' hours, we're still doing it. It all counts.

And if someone questions your choices, I can highly recommend answering through the medium of poetry. I promise you, they won't do it again.

What Do You Want to Do with Your Life?

She's like, yeah,
but what do you want to *do* with your life?
And I'm like, uh
(clutching my pearls),
I don't know how to tell you this...

I want to plant a tree and watch it grow for eighty years,
just so I can write it a thank-you note
for the oxygen and the shade.
(And probably also apologise
for all the paper I've wasted.)
I want to eat spoonfuls of mac and cheese
in spite of my lactose intolerance.
I want to be a morning person,
but also stay up all night having long, existential chats
with the stars.

I want to take the scenic route.
I want to use my whole heart.
I want to not immediately get out of the car
but sit for a second after we've parked,
watching the rain make rivers on the glass.

I want to fall in love with my own bad ideas,
like the time I tried to bake a cake
with an entire thingy of cinnamon,
then had the audacity to pretend I did it on purpose,
presented it to the table
as a *commentary on indulgence*
when, in fact,
it was just disgusting.

I want to run into the sea
like a woman in a perfume ad,

stay until my skin wrinkles,
dry off in a café with
half-written poems in my notebook
and a half-healed heart in my chest.

I want to fall in love
with learning how to get back up again,
ask the rivers to teach me how they hold both
fury and stillness,
what does it mean
to carry everything and then let it all go.

I want to watch bad TV,
and laugh so much
I forget the sharp edges of the day.
I want to be someone who remembers things,
like birthdays
and my mum's quiche recipe
and the sound of my dad shouting *Jorge!!* through the static,
distant but clear.

I want to keep asking questions, like
why do we tell ourselves we're too old for certain things?
Why am I still paying £8.99 a month
for a meditation app I haven't opened since 2020?
Why can I still remember every lyric
to 'One Night Stand' by Mis-Teeq,
and 'Doctor Jones' by Aqua
and 'Rock the Boat' by the Hues Corporation,
which I literally only overheard a handful of times while I was
rehearsing for the Deeping Gang Show
when I was about thirteen?
Why does tea taste better when someone else makes it?
Why are straight men on dating apps so obsessed with fish?
Why is it a bad thing to be seen Repeating An Outfit?
Why do we whisper the things we're proud of
and scream the things we regret?

And then she blinks at me
and says, *Yeah, that's, like, quite a lot.*
I just meant, like, work wise.

I smile. I know.
But the honest answer to her question
is that I do want it all,
because I'm so in love with the loud, messy wonder
of even being here at all,
so give me
every bruise, every bloom,
every impossible thing.

Acknowledgements

Thank you to Clive and Kate at Burning Eye, for believing in me enough to give this a go.

To Jack Kenyon, for the cover. And for the picture of Peter, who now sits in my loo with his big onion: overseer of ablutions and heartbreak baths (poor thing).

To Harriet Evans, for becoming my teammate in what is otherwise a fairly solo (and strangely vulnerable) expedition into the weird woods of Making A Book. Thank you for caring so much, for your wise little nudges and for never once writing *sorry, what is wrong with you*, which I consider to be heroic restraint. Thank you also for volunteering the diameter of your areola grandes, a task which undoubtedly lies outside your job description. Turns out, when you've got good people in your corner, even the most bizarre anxieties can just melt away.

To Mum and Dad, for an entire lifetime of support, for clapping even when you brought your friends to a gig where I repeatedly used the word *minge*. You never once said *do you think you should have a backup plan*, you just let me believe I could do this, and, even more incredibly, you believed it too. Thank you a million times.

To Smavs, for being the first published poet in the family and setting the bar so high. For coming to all the gigs and reminding me to trust my own voice, even when it's shaking.

To Scrimby, for your willingness to come along for the ride. By which I quite literally mean the drive across the UK while I rehearse the same fifteen-minute set over and over again, like a deranged podcast host with only one episode. For your patience, for the *yeah, girlies*, for being the soft place I land.

To Harry Baker, for sharing your time, knowledge and platform so generously.

To everybody who's watched a video, shared a snippet, come to a gig or told me that you *don't usually like poetry, but...*, you are the reason this thing you're holding exists outside my notes app. Not to be dramatic, but you're the reason I get to do what I love. Thank you. I owe you, big time.

www.ingramcontent.com/pod-product-compliance
Lightning Source LLC
La Vergne TN
LVHW092004080726
842905LV00026B/225
9781913958510